Starting
Fabric Collage

Frances Kay

Studio Vista London
Watson-Guptill Publications New York

For Virginia, Sarah and James

General Editors Janey O'Riordan and Brenda Herbert
© Frances Kay 1969
Published in London by Studio Vista Limited
Blue Star House, Highgate Hill, London N19
and in New York by Watson-Guptill Publications
165 West 46th Street, New York 10036
Library of Congress Catalog Card Number 69-13171
Distributed in Canada by General Publishing Co. Ltd
30 Lesmill Road, Don Mills, Toronto, Canada
Set in Univers 9 on 9½ point
by V. Siviter Smith and Co. Ltd, Birmingham
Printed in the Netherlands
by N. V. Grafische Industrie Haarlem
SBN 289 79579 6

Starting Fabric Collage

Contents

Acknowledgements

The author would like to thank Mr and Mrs R. H. Potter for permission to reproduce 'The Puffing Potter' on the cover and frontispiece.

The author and publishers would like to make the following acknowledgements for pictures in this book:

Cover and fig. 51: photographs by Deste; figs. 9, 25, 40, 86: photographs by Ledbetter of Leeds, Ltd; figs. 17, 77, 78: photographs by John Minshall; fig. 76: photograph by Mark Gerson; fig. 79: photograph by Warwick Hutton; fig. 80: photograph by W. G. Belsher, A.R.P.S. All the other photographs were taken by T. Ryder.

Introduction

Fabric collage is simply the art of sticking pieces of material on to a backing to form a picture.

The word 'collage' comes from the French verb 'coller', to paste or glue. The word 'fabric' is usually allowed to cover not only textiles, but metal thread, feathers, 'jewels', shells, butterflies' wings and occasional paper and painting. But to be fabric collage it must be mainly fabric. You can stretch the term to cover a picture in which some stitching is used to decorate or reinforce the fabrics, but if the picture is mainly put together with needle and thread, then it isn't fabric collage, it is embroidery.

All this shows how elastic our terms are. This is in accord with the feeling of an age which says there are no frontiers in art. It does also allow the individual great scope to stretch the medium to suit himself. This is the perfect medium for the person weary of reproductions who wants to create something entirely personal and original to hang on his walls.

Compared with embroidery, fabric collage is a very modern art. With more and more exciting and varied textiles, as well as reliable glues, coming on the market, it has great potential. At a time when some people feel many forms of art have developed almost as far as they can go, fabric collage is comparatively just beginning. This is very exciting. I don't know anybody who has worked in this medium who has not found it at least fun — and occasionally invested with a touch of magic.

1 History of fabric collage

Fabric collage as a recognised medium for making pictures has not had a long history. Even today, many artists are not inclined to take it seriously as an art form, but there are honourable exceptions to this viewpoint — Picasso, for instance.

To paste things up as a decoration to one's home is a fairly basic instinct. In fig. 1 I have pictured a very early bit of cave collage as it might have happened. The female partner has forsaken the cooking, to fasten up the hide of a three-toed, curly-tusked, woolly-matted wart-hog and the man, returning hungry from the hunt, is not entirely appreciative! Nowadays everything is better managed.

To move from the world of speculation to the world we know; fabric collage leads gradually into embroidery and is becoming an increasingly greater force in the world of pictures as its possibilities are realised. Also the greater reliability of glues today has something to do with it. In the seventeenth century, English stump work mingled embroidery and sticking (gluing) in a three dimensional way which aimed at a primitive kind of realism, and there are examples of religious work found in Austria which combine the two techniques. But while gluing might serve as a technique for the isolated individual, it was never cultivated and taught until this century.

Fig. 1 Cave Collage

8

In the last century in Britain and America, there were a number of gifted leisured ladies. Most of them took up watercolour painting, piano-playing or ballad singing, but a very few tried their hand at something quite different. Among the few was Mrs Dickson who copied a painting by Poussin, using tailor's cuttings and glue with a very few stitches, (fig. 2). It was exhibited at Brighton in 1831, just too late for the Prince Regent's eye to see and appreciate. I feel that the taste which inspired the Brighton Pavilion would have appreciated the possibilities of fabric collage.

Other ladies at this time were making fruit and flower pictures or doing Bible scenes in fabric. The results that were framed and have survived were usually charming, sometimes eccentric. They usually combined gluing and stitching. I fancy they probably made their own glues in the kitchen and may not have had complete faith in their own produce and hence reinforced it with stitches.

Another slightly offbeat form of decoration that some ladies went in for was dressing prints. They cut out fashion prints from their journals and then clothed the paper figures with muslins, lawns or whatever seemed appropriate to the fashion.

Fig. 2 Setting Sun, after Poussin, by Mrs Dickson (Courtesy Victoria and Albert Museum, London)

Fig. 3 Two unidentified ladies at Midgham House, the seat of W. S. Poyntz, Esq.
M.P. *c.*1840

I possess a dressed print of a kind (fig. 3), dating from about 1840, which, the back tells me, shows Midgham House, the seat of W. S. Poyntz, Esq. M.P. There is no mention of who the two ladies with their poodle and pug, walking from their shell grotto towards the house, may be. Perhaps one is a self-portrait of the artist. The picture ingeniously combines a print of the house, hand watercoloured, a freely painted foreground, a great variety of real shells stuck on to what looks as though it might be the defunct spine of a book, and a corded 'mount' for the setting. The dogs are painted on paper, cut out and glued to the picture in relief. Emily and Wilhemina Poyntz (or whatever their names were) are clothed in muslins and narrow ribbons which form costumes of the early Victorian period.

Anyone, with a little ingenuity, could do the same sort of thing today, showing themselves and their home, but there are now far wider possibilities for putting together fabrics with glue to make pictures. People are making exciting abstracts, exploiting the chance to combine pure colour, texture and form to create a new kind of picture. In the wide territory between straight representation and abstract, fig. 4 shows Kathleen Whyte's imaginative treatment of filmy textures forming diaphanous flowers, set between two transparent sheets of perspex. This is just one of the ways in which you can make fabric collage pictures today, and in the course of this book I shall show many others.

Fig. 4 Poppies, by Kathleen Whyte (Courtesy Victoria and Albert Museum, London)

2 Finding materials

The finding of materials for fabric collage is so much a creative part of the picture-making that I have put it even before 'Sources of inspiration'. So often the material itself is the source of inspiration. You start your picture the minute you consciously start looking for materials for it, so it is quite unlike buying paint to start a painting. Nobody is likely to come back from the shops exulting: 'I've found the most wonderful tube of yellow ochre!' in the way that they may crow over the discovery of some gold velvet to represent a monarch's robe.

Actually buying the materials is probably the least rewarding way of collecting them and, without being sentimental about it, I think new material does lack a certain patina acquired by used materials. The best treasures come from scraps hoarded from dressmaking and upholstery, or inherited from old ladies' work boxes, or simply scrounged from kind friends. Almost no piece is too insignificant to be worth preserving, provided it is not filthy. The Woolworth string of pearls that came to pieces may be just what you need to highlight a moonlit swan, while a few inches of silver lace from an old lady's workbag shadow his wings (fig. 5). Or an old crochet mat might turn into architectural fan tracery, or a piece of gift-wrapping gold cord be just what is needed for an angel's halo. Half the fun of collage is the magic transformation one can effect on a commonplace scrap.

Supposing you decided to do a version of Adam and Eve in the garden of Eden, it would be difficult, if not impossible, to go and buy all at once the materials you need. Try asking a shop assistant for some material that looks like a serpent's skin, and then study her face!

For the impatient, who do not want to wait until they have hoarded materials, I shall describe in chapter 4 one or two pictures whose raw materials could be quite easily purchased from any ordinary fabric store. For the rest, I hope you will believe that collecting your hoard is half the fun and three quarters of the inspiration.

When you do shop, choose the shops where the goods are laid out like a bazaar and you can wander around inspecting things thoughtfully, without having to ask the assistant's help before making a choice. Haunt any open air markets where they sell fabrics. There, not only will you be able to examine the pattern closely, but they will be cheap. Also some textile mills have shops attached to them where they sell off slightly spoiled rolls of fabric at bargain prices. Remember, for collage purposes a fault in the printing or weaving is no disaster. It has been known to be an

Fig. 5 Moonlit Swan (Courtesy Mr and Mrs J. Saunders)

Fig. 6 Cockerel by Frances Kay (Courtesy Major A. C. Eyre)

asset. Do not scorn jumble (rummage) sales, they can yield astonishing treasure for practically no outlay.

If you know any dressmakers and upholsterers, cultivate their friendship. They can be the source of the most wonderful scraps. Quite tiny pieces can be useful; pieces that would otherwise go straight into their waste-paper baskets. In this connection, collect any pattern books and sample swatches that you can get hold of; some friendly shops are prepared to let you have them as they fall out of date, either free or for a small sum. The swatches may be only 6" × 4", or even smaller, but it is surprising how much you can do with them, especially when you get a subtle range of different shades of one material. It was a small swatch of slub silks in blues, greens, red and gold that started me off on a cockerel (young rooster) (fig. 6). Almost every collagist seems impelled to do a cockerel at some time. The flamboyant flourish of their tail feathers is irresistible (see figs. 7–10).

Just thinking about how difficult it is to paint transparent substances, makes one enthusiastic about the use of net in collage. It is invitingly cheap and fascinating to use. Net can represent smoke (fig. 11), foam (fig. 12), clouds or romantic atmosphere (fig. 13), shadows (fig. 14, which does not pretend to demonstrate correct perspective), ghosts (fig. 16); or it can delineate contours (fig. 15) or cover the whole scene in mist or duskiness.

Cockerels
Fig. 7 by Vera Sherman
Fig. 8 by Eugenie Alexander
Fig. 9 by Margaret Connor
Fig. 10 by Margaret Kaye
(Courtesy Roland, Browse and
Delbanco, London)

Fig. 11 Bonfire
Fig. 12 *Golden Hind* in a storm
Fig. 13 Cliffside, by Eugenie Alexander
Fig. 14 Desert Pillar

By partially covering one coloured net with another you can get subtle gradations of colour. I find the old silk or cotton nets are much easier to bunch, the new nylon nets are easier to lay flat. For the impressionist, net or the slightly thicker tarlatan are invaluable for building up atmosphere. You will have gathered that I am enthusiastic about the use of net! In chapter 6 there will be instructions for gluing it down, without having to hold it with stitches.

Cottonwool (absorbent cotton) can also provide smoke (see frontispiece), clouds and snow, but it is not the easiest of materials to apply without the glue showing through.

If you can find any shaded materials, fall on them. Shaded materials go from dark tones to light across the material from selvage to selvage, or sometimes shade into another colour in mid warp. They are known technically as 'ombré' and, as you can imagine, there is not much demand for them in dressmaking, so they are difficult to find. However, they open up a wealth of possibilities in collage. In fig. 11 I used a chiffon scarf, shaded from black to white, over bright blue repp (transversely corded fabric) for the background. Used over brilliant orange cotton, it has also made a menacing sky. Shaded blue satin, used either on its matt or shiny side, makes a very convincing sky as it pales towards the horizon. Of course you can experiment with bleaching off or dyeing parts of a plain material, perhaps an old sheet, but it is not at all easy to do consistently.

Fig. 17 Self Portrait (36" × 48") by Tim Jones, Hornsey College of Art

Tim Jones, a fashion textiles student, dyed white felt to flesh tones for his monumental self-portrait (fig. 17). He also designed the background material himself. Felt is one of the great stand-bys in collage, especially for beginners, as it is so easy to handle, will not fray, and does not let the glue show through. It can be used for the simplest shapes, like a ball or crescent moon cut out by a six-year-old, or it can be used as subtly as Tim Jones has done.

Ribbons, braids, especially narrow russian braids, fringes, cords, lace, embroidery silks and wools, beads, feathers and sequins can all embellish your pictures to tremendous effect. Anne Carpenter has used some beads and a piece of old lace to give a witty flourish to her picture of a 'bright young thing' (fig. 18).

18

Fig. 18 Bright Young Thing, by Anne Carpenter (Courtesy Heal's, London)
Fig. 19 Field Officer, Welsh Guards, by Charles Hammick

Charles Hammick, an ex-Guards Officer himself, has been fastidious in getting every detail right in his picture of a Field Officer (Staff), Welsh Guards, in present day Guard of Honour order (fig. 19). To get his braids, cords etc exactly right he goes to eight different sources. As he sells to many forces and ex-forces people, he has to be exactly correct. Imagination boggles at the apoplexy which might be caused if the tunics were wrongly buttoned! This is not, however, the kind of worry which need concern most people doing fabric collage. If you want to have a shaggy snake, have one; if you want to have a magenta sky, patterned in green lilies, by all means do. The disciplines imposed by fabric collage are disciplines of technique, not of expression.

Storing

Supposing you have been magnetically successful in collecting, this is where chaos ensues unless you are careful. You must have a system for storing materials, if you are not to waste hours looking through all your treasures for the essential scrap you are absolutely certain you remember seeing somewhere. I suggest transparent polythene (polyethelene) bags are the best answer. They are expensive to buy in quantity, but as so many clothes are now bought contained in them, one can soon make a collection of assorted sizes. I use separate bags for each colour, with another bag for striped, checked or spotted materials, another for floral prints, and perhaps others for glittering materials, furry ones and so on. Or you may devise much better classifications for yourself. If you want to specialise in your subjects, you will not need so wide a range anyway. With this method you can see quickly the range you have to choose from. Ideally, you should be able at once to put your hands on the stuff for say, a flamingo's wing or a matador's cloak. But of course, the ideal doesn't always happen. Time spent rooting through your fabrics need not be time wasted, if you take mental note of what you are rooting through. Inspiration may come from such a search.

If you keep braids, ribbons and fringes semi-detached in their own small bags within the colour-schemed bags, you are less likely to have a collection looking like spaghetti bolognaise. But don't despair if your ribbons get knotted and fabrics get crushed, a minute with the iron before you use them will cure the crushed look; though just occasionally, perhaps for a rocky mountain, crumpling can be a positive asset.

Where you keep all your transparent bags is going to depend largely on the long-suffering people you live with. A note of encouragement: a huge volume of stuff can be crushed into a smallish cupboard, if you are prepared to use an iron afterwards. But if these bags are not to encroach too much on your living space, you will have to exercise some selectivity. I would not, for instance, suggest that you collect all your old nylon stockings, unless you have some very special project in mind—such as a moon landscape. But on the whole, nylon is one of the less sympathetic materials to use.

As a principle, hoard just as many pieces as you can control and the other people in your home will tolerate. Nobody is going to pretend that fabric collage will help the tidiness of the home, and small domestic pets are apt to misinterpret the object of such

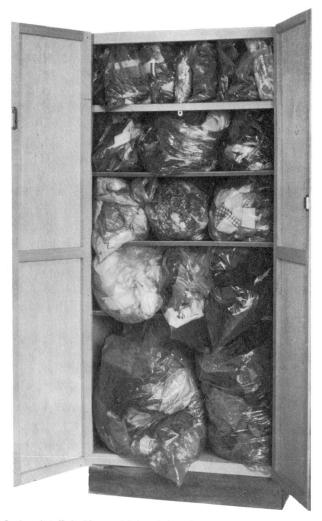

Fig. 20 Cupboard stuffed with materials in polythene bags

a collection, but it's still worth it. If you hoard your treasures, sort them, pore over them and memorize them; then when you start a picture, they will prove a gold mine, not an avalanche to overwhelm you.

Equipment and backing materials

Essential equipment for fabric collage is minimal. You could start work with a pair of nail scissors, a tube of glue and a piece of cardboard to act as backing, but life would be easier with a few other things as well.

In fig. 21 I have shown the equipment I use. Probably the most controversial item is the backing material. I like to use pelmet-weight vilene (pellon) as a backing for my pictures. It is firm enough, but can be stitched through if you want to add stitching. You may prefer to start with cardboard which would be cheaper. Some people like to use hardboard for their backing. It comes to much the same cost as the heavyweight vilene (pellon). When using hardboard, you may like to use one basic background material and, instead of gluing it down, lace it tautly over the hardboard at the back, from top to bottom and side to side. If a large expanse of the background is to show, it will probably lie flatter if it is laced than if it is glued. Another advantage of hardboard is that it can easily be propped up rigidly to judge the work in progress; a disadvantage is that work on hardboard can only be stitched with a curved needle. Another disadvantage is that you cannot easily change the size or shape of your picture, once you have begun on hardboard; vilene (pellon) can be added to at the back, or very easily trimmed.

Some people prefer to use canvas or sailcloth as a backing and tack it to a frame while working. Millionaires may like to use canvases prepared for oil paintings. You may prefer to do away with the need for a backing and buy the kind of hessian (burlap) which is treated to act as wall-covering, as a background on its own. It comes in a good range of colours, but it is not cheap. Alternatively you may like to use felt; either thick carpet felt, or the thinner kind that you can buy in a vast range of colours. Felt or hessian (burlap) can each play the part of backing and background in one, for a simple picture. Some examples of this are shown in chapter 4.

Beware of thin materials for backing; when the framer glues them to hardboard, the glue may come through to the face and show disastrously.

I have several pairs of pointed scissors, including a large pair for cutting out the vilene (pellon). It is a help to have two or three smaller pairs, so that time is not wasted hunting for the one which may get lost among the fabrics. The same goes for glue spreaders, which come with the glue. I hoard them so that I always have several available. I use Copydex glue (Elmer's or Sobo in the U.S.)

Fig. 21 Equipment needed

in a tube. I know other people who prefer Bateman's, Uhu, Evo-stick and Bostick. Whichever you pick, choose one which will peel off your fingers as Copydex does. It can also be scratched off the front of smooth materials. Glue can be bought at any good stationers or hardware shop.

The paper-weight (fig. 21) is to anchor materials after they have been glued; pins hold trial pieces in place on the background while I consider them, held vertically, and the tweezers are used to pick up delicate pieces.

I bought the set-square at the behest of my framer who was tired of trying to frame pictures which were not right-angled at the corners. The ruler also helps me to present the pictures with something like straight sides too. The sketching pad with felt pen and pencil are for preliminary rough sketches. The iron explains itself. If you reckon that you have an iron anyway, the outlay on equipment is thus not great.

3 Sources of inspiration

As I have said, it is difficult to decide whether to start with the subject inspiration for a picture, or the materials for it, so interdependent are they on each other. The germ of the picture may simply be a desire to do something original. Nobody needs to strive too hard for originality in fabric collage. It would be a good deal more difficult to produce an exact copy of an existing fabric collage, than to produce an original one, and in the unlikely event of a class of collage students having to reproduce a still-life arrangement of dishes and fruit in fabric, they would probably all produce very different results.

I think it would be true to say that collagists with some training in art are more prepared to specialise in subject-matter than are the self-taught like myself, who usually like exploring for themselves in all directions. I was trained for two years in needlework at a rather old-fashioned establishment. Perhaps that is why I never use any stitching in my work now! But I do not regret all the training I received there. It left me with an excited sense of the possibilities of fabric, and great impatience. I did not stay the full course and eventually came to fabric collage in middle age, via interior decoration and resident work in historic homes open to the public. The last was probably the most formative influence: I was surrounded by things both beautiful and very individual. As a source of inspiration, historic homes and, if they will forgive me, their owners, are inexhaustible.

I have always liked filing away illustrations from newspapers, brochures and catalogues that appealed to me, and I suggest that, if you do not already do this, you should start now. These, together with your own personal photographs, can provide you with a fund of ideas and a reference library: when you need to check on a Red Indian's war paint, the patterning of a zebra or the architecture of the Taj Mahal, then you apply to your files.

But this is not to suggest that you should copy straight from your filed illustrations. As an exercise, I set myself to copy in fabric an old Mughal painting from the Victoria and Albert Museum. I reproduce here the original (fig. 22) and the collage (fig. 23) to show what is lost in simply trying to copy. Paradoxically, the quality most conspicuously absent in the fabric picture is the swirl and freedom in the skirts and saris that the original so marvellously captured. So your illustrations are for inspiration and for guidance, not for copying.

An art which may put on display pieces of your own old clothing is bound to be personal, so you may like to start with a very personal subject for a picture, such as a family wedding, possibly

Fig. 22 Kathak Dancers—old Mughal painting (Courtesy Victoria and Albert Museum)
Fig. 23 Fabric copy of fig 22

using small pieces left over from the actual dresses portrayed. Don't worry too much about likenesses; you can make a character recognisable first with the clothes and then with a slight exaggeration of figure and hairstyle.

Humour happens naturally in collage. Sometimes it is unintentional, as when a piece of material is easily recognisable from quite another context, and this will deter most people from attempting tragic subjects in fabric collage. A familiar piece of household stuff would be too distracting in a theme such as the crucifixion. On the other hand, it would add to the amusement in a picture of a clown.

A good example of a theme deeply felt, but still highly suitable for fabric collage, is Mary Ffrench's 'Master Race' (fig. 24). She shows the heavy tread of civilisation about to stamp out the rest of nature. This kind of apocryphal subject, in which the Bible too is particularly rich, lends itself marvellously to fabric. It was used extensively by the late Miss Elizabeth Allen in her fascinating stitched rag pictures. She was discovered and publicised as 'England's Grandma Moses'.

Another quite different but very appropriate source of inspiration is shown by Margaret Connor's picture, 'The Bridge' (fig. 25): namely, the scene around us. Margaret Connor lives in Yorkshire, and draws deeply on the urban industrial cities of the north of England for her very effective pictures. She has recognised that there is inherent drama in the juxtaposed shapes of office sky-scrapers, industrial 'coolers', factory chimneys and church spires. Margaret Connor is an inspired teacher too, as the work of her young pupils shows (see fig. 40). Both she and Mary Ffrench are natural self-taught artists and both have the gift of the seeing eye.

If you are going to depict scenery, either urban or rustic, or just your own home, you will probably find that a camera, preferably loaded with colour film, is a very great help indeed. You can hardly take your collage, as you can your sketchbook, on a picnic. This is just as well, because collage demands a degree of simpli-fication and abstraction from the scene, which is not best obtained when you are surrounded by the landscape itself. Try to take faithful photographs and then distil the essence of the scene from them.

Angela Steveni, who has been inspired by the work of the architect Vanbrugh, is a good example of an artist who can extract the essence of a scene. Fig. 26 shows a gateway in the grand manner. This picture was not in fact specifically inspired by Vanbrugh, but it seems to me imbued with his baroque style. Angela Steveni feeds her supply of inspiration with constant visits to Blenheim Palace, Castle Howard and other houses designed by Vanbrugh.

On a more mundane level, you may find travel brochures help-ful with their bright simplified symbols for the star places: New York (Statue of Liberty), Athens (the Parthenon), Pisa (the Leaning Tower) — and so on. But your own photographs are even better. A collage of your own most memorable holiday could be a composite montage, combining the different places you visited. Perhaps the very hot places could be shown behind a 'heat-haze' of applied net, or, if you celebrated enthusiastically on the wine

Fig. 24 Master Race, by Mary Ffrench
Fig. 25 The Bridge, by Margaret Connor (Courtesy Trustees, Kay-Shuttleworth Collection, Gawthorpe Hall)

Fig. 26 The Gateway, by Angela Steveni (Courtesy Trustees, Kay-Shuttleworth Collection, Gawthorpe Hall)

of the country, a hint of double vision could be introduced. Or perhaps you will show yourself mingling with sheikhs, or grappling with sharks. If personal fiction is ethically dubious, a little suggestion is perfectly permissible in collage. By all means put in the summit of the mountain you got about half way up. Fabric collage releases one into a world where fantasy is the normal order of things, and this can include every aspect of one's rose-tinted (or brow-beaten) childhood.

If you want to get beyond the personal in your pictures, then there is the whole of history for you to draw on. An epic, such as Custer's Last Stand, has become legendary enough for the tragic implications to have been softened. The theatre, opera, ballet, the race-track, royal and presidential occasions, pageantry, and even politics, can all provide inspiration in plenty.

I have so far been making suggestions for a purely figurative way of working. But it is possible that many people will find

Fig. 27 Barnacled stone

Fig. 28 Abstract, inspired
by barnacled stone,
by Audrey Thorne

their greatest inspiration in forms which suggest abstract pictures. At present most of the fabric work in art schools is abstract in form, but there are signs that the pendulum is swinging away from complete absorbtion in the abstract. Personally I think both forms are necessary and complementary and need not compete with each other.

Unless their concept of an abstract is completely geometric, most people find inspiration for abstracts from some form of natural life: it may be from the elements— water and fire particularly suggest wonderful forms; it could be from the cross-section of a cabbage or an onion, or even the biological pattern of molecular cells. In chapter 8 there are a number of examples. Here, fig. 27 shows a barnacled stone picked up on the sea-shore, and in fig. 28 you can see how Audrey Thorne has used it to produce a very disciplined, cool abstract that conveys the natural forms without slavishly copying them. She has found inspiration from sources as varied as computer tape and swans in flight. There are no limits to the supply of ideas if you can learn to use your eyes and make a note of anything that interests or excites you.

4 First steps in simple collage

Supposing you want to try your hand at fabric collage, before you have had time to form much of a collection of bits and pieces, you can buy the few materials you need for a first simple picture at any ordinary fabric store. You can easily stock up the other essential equipment mentioned in chapter 2.

For the backing, you may decide to use wall hessian (burlap) as in fig. 30, or you can start off by sticking your fabrics on to coloured carboard as in fig. 29. In this gay little picture, Margaret Gregory has used only five different remnants of material—and a lot of imagination.

You may prefer to use felt for your backing/background. It can be bought up to 72" wide, which will suit those whose ideas are on a large scale. It is very easy to handle, will not fray, will not let the glue through to the face and so is eminently suitable for this type of simple picture. In fig. 31 Georgina Hammick, with the trained artist's eye for line, has used felt with scraps of tweed, fringe and lace to great effect for a perfect nursery picture. In fig. 32 she has done a slightly more elaborate picture with tremendous verve to it. Part of its charm is in the way the few materials are used in the most telling way; nothing is lost in fuss.

This kind of picture is a greater test of design than of applying the materials, so you will probably want to work out your design carefully on paper first, before committing yourself to buying materials.

It is perhaps best to start by producing the kind of picture that appeals to the very young, and to choose your subject accordingly. Animals probably come first to mind, and cows, lions, hamsters, kangaroos, etc, can all be made into genial decorations for a child's room. Or you may prefer to go back to pre-history for a woolly mammoth or a dinosaur. Simple objects like crackers and balloons also have an immediate appeal. Don't try to give your picture an elaborate background; keep the shapes bold and clear and the colour scheme bright.

Fig. 29 The Dance on the Bridge, by Margaret Gregory
Fig. 30 Flamingo
Fig. 31 Hobby Horse, by Georgina Hammick
Fig. 32 Victorian Doll's Pram, by Georgina Hammick

Fig. 29

The dance on the Bridge

Fig. 30/31

Fig. 32

31

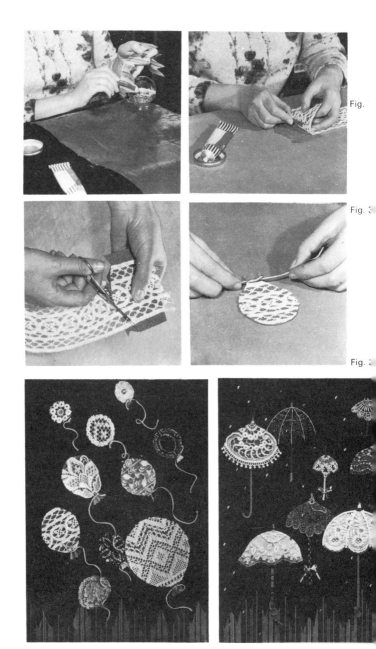

Making a simple nursery picture

This picture of balloons could have for its background cardboard, wall-hessian (burlap), or fabric stuck on vilene (pellon), preferably blue to suggest the sky. I happened to have a piece of blue PVC (vinyl) available, so I used this stuck on vilene (pellon). It is not ideal, as PVC does not stay glued as reliably as other materials do and it is a bit shiny. Sticking the background fabric to the backing is one of the trickiest processes of all, (see chapter 6), so I suggest you start this picture on an all-in-one background/backing, such as felt.

Fig. 33 To suggest grass, I have cut out some blue and green striped PVC (vinyl) with irregular points. This is applied by putting the glue onto the 'grass' with the spreader, then anchoring it to the background with a paperweight (or any other heavy object) to hold it in place while sticking. Practically always you should apply the glue to the piece to be stuck, not to the background, as it is difficult to judge exactly where on the base to apply the glue. The exception to this is when applying lace, beads, or other microscopically small pieces.

Fig. 34 To make the balloons, take some gaily coloured material in contrast to the background colour. I have chosen orange textured PVC (vinyl) which cannot fray. (I had a sample book of these textured PVCs in gay colours which proved ideal. Any cotton or smooth surfaced material would do for this picture, preferably plain, though a small design would not matter if it did not war with the lace design.) Choose a scrap of boldly patterned lace. Apply the glue to the lace and stick it to the balloon base material, leaving a little uncovered to form the neck of the balloon. You can either choose pieces of lace with a definite round design, or you can be more haphazard with the lace. I have tried to get my lace patterns centred on my balloons, but this is not essential.

Fig. 35 When the lace is firmly stuck down, cut the two fabrics together into a balloon shape. I tried different shaped balloons, but in the end decided round ones were best.

Fig. 36 Tie a short piece of cord or narrow ribbon round the neck of each balloon, leaving a few inches of cord at one end.

Fig. 37 Arrange your balloons for their fly-past by first pinning them to the picture, which should then be propped or pinned vertically, so that you can stand away from it. Do not stick them down until you are satisfied with the design. To suggest distance, I have put the small ones near the top where they would be highest, or behind the bigger ones. Stick down the balloons and

cords, being careful to arrange the cords behind or in front of other balloons, according to their position in 'the air'.
Fig. 38 A variation on the balloon theme, with umbrellas. Here the lace has to be more carefully chosen and placed to suggest the shape of the umbrella. Silver sequins were cut up to make the rain drops. The glue was dropped in tiny blobs onto the picture where I wanted rain drops and then the sequins were applied with tweezers. Applying glue to sequins direct is one quick way of going mad!

Family collage

To prove that you need absolutely no previous experience in fabric collage to produce an amusing nursery picture, I persuaded my brother, his wife and their three children to do one. The result was 'Any number can play!' (fig. 39). Sarah and James (aged 12 and 8) had tried their hand at it before, but the adults' only collage experience was confined to mending household things with insulating tape and sticking on adhesive name tapes.

Their picture shows mother's elephant on the left, with the characteristic mothers' touch of knotted tail to jog its elephantine memory. It is in far the best taste, with rather elegant trappings of gold and black, and 'diamond' toenails. Next is James's low-slung model, an interesting new breed built for sport. In the middle is 16-year-old Virginia's elephant: rather rude and distinctly over-weight; this one least reflects its maker. Next is Sarah's mini-model, a lovable creature with genuinely Indian trappings. Last is father's 'introverted hypochondriac' elephant—an interesting 'case'.

I found I had to provide them with plenty of pencils, pairs of scissors, glue spreaders and more than one tube of glue. Co-operative efforts are fine in collage, as long as there is plenty of equipment: 'After you with the scissors', 'Hey, who's swiped the spreader?' and that sort of talk is bad for artistic concentration. I also managed to clear them a good deal of space at a large table.

I had found them plenty of wrinkly-looking grey PVC (vinyl), which I knew would not fray, for the elephant hide. They outlined their elephants on the back of this with pencil, but they had to be reminded that if you drew it facing right on the reverse, it would face left when the material was turned over. Ears were cut out and applied separately and James's elephant, which always was a bit like a pantomime horse, had at one stage quite detached rear and front ends. I think the family were surprised how flexible the

Fig. 39 Any Number can Play!, by the Kay family

medium of fabric collage can be. Some black sequins were found for eyes, white artificial leather for tusks, grey russian braid for tails and, for Virginia, some transparent plastic for her elephant's water spout. They enjoyed digging into the trimmings bags to find appropriate trappings and every elephant got equipped without terrible clashing of colour schemes.

I had started off the project with the innocent idea that all the elephants would be in procession one behind the other, but I had reckoned without the stubborn individualism of the people involved. It proved, in the event, quite difficult to fit this herd onto the allotted length of vilene (pellon). But they jostled on and we set them off against a blue sky and a purple ground, because they did not seem to be the sort of elephants who called for a natural-istic setting. The whole picture was bordered in purple braid and, since nobody was prepared to invest money in framing it, it was slung by braid loops on to a bamboo stick. A purple dressing-gown cord, attached to either end of the bamboo, was used to hang it from a ribbon covered hook. Hung in the children's play room, I should think its physical life will last about as long as it will continue to entertain people – perhaps a year.

Hints on method for simple pictures

For your first picture, choose a simple, bold subject.

Sketch it out on paper about the size you intend the finished subject to be.

Choose a backing—vilene (pellon), cardboard, hardboard, treated hessian (burlap), or whatever else you prefer—that is amply big for your design. You can always trim it down afterwards, you cannot easily add to it. Designs have a tendency to grow in the making.

Choose thick rather than thin materials, as they will not let the glue come through to the face.

Choose cottons, rather than silks, as they are more likely to be firm and less likely to fray when you don't want them to. If a material is just the colour and texture you want, but insists on undisciplined fraying, iron it onto thin, adhesive vilene first and this should cure the fraying. You will probably find that jersey materials are particularly co-operative about not fraying.

Always judge the progress of your picture when it is in a vertical position. Pin your pieces onto the backing and then pin the picture either to a wall, or to the back of an upholstered chair or sofa. If you are doubtful about the picture, leave it pinned up for a while and then come back and surprise it.

Be comfortable to work. Sit down if you can. If you stoop over the picture, you will in the end get backache and this will colour your feelings about the picture! Some people like to work on a slight incline, as at a school desk.

Have a good light. Of course daylight is much the best, but if you want to work at night, have a strong light angled over your shoulder.

Pictures will look entirely different by different lights. This applies to fabric pictures even more than to paintings, because of the way different textures catch the light to different degrees. It is part of the excitement of the medium.

If you have not caught the effect you want, don't cling to a piece of material in the design just because you can't bear the thought of wasting an expensive piece of fabric. It will be more expensive if it spoils the picture. You can usually rip a piece off, or cover it up with another piece, without revealing any hint of a mistake in the finished picture. I have a bag full of rejects, like angels' wings and bits of lion, that part of me is convinced will be just what I want some day. Of course they never will, but they are a valuable object-lesson.

Remember you must begin the picture with the background. If it is a landscape, the sky will come first. You might be able to paint sky between the tracery of a tree's branches, but you certainly cannot stick sky to a collage in this way. Work strictly from the distance towards the foreground of the picture. Elementary perhaps, but easily forgotten.

Ideas for simple pictures

Variations on the elephant picture, which might include any group of animals wearing gay trappings, such as camels or donkeys.

Any animals with bold recognisable shapes, cut out in fabric with a small printed pattern and put in procession, going into a simple ark, or behind wide thin bars in a zoo. Jungles are more difficult and need experience.

Trees, houses, castles, churches, butterflies — anything with a bold recognisable shape, can be cut out in fabric with a small pattern and made into a design.

Clothes hanging up on a clothes line. Against blue sky fabric, a fine cord makes the clothes line. The clothes can be cut out in interesting shapes from appropriate material, such as lace for a nightdress, fine jersey for long pants, etc.

A water lily. Dark blue water, smooth green leaves, white satin petals and yellow russian braid frayed out for the stamens.

An orchard in blossom, using brown felt to make the trunks and branches and white lace to make the blossom.

Portrait of a favourite toy.

Sailing boat on a calm sea; later, when you are more experienced, sailing boat on a rough sea!

A covered wagon or gypsy caravan.

Fireworks, using sequins of different colours on a dark ground.

A clown or other circus artist.

Almost any underwater scenes. The net or other transparent material used for the water not only adds mysterious quality to the picture but covers up defects such as obtrusive glue beneath. Underwater scenes might show a wrecked sailing ship, spilling treasure in the shape of gold sequins, or any fish with an interesting shape and colour — and some of them are fabulous. Or you might try a drowned church, suggesting the lost city of Atlantis.

5 Working with children

One of the nicest things about fabric collage is that it can be as co-operative as a kibbutz: much more easily so than painting. It is also a happy medium for the old and the young to work in together — not a take-over bid by an adult 'helping' a child, but a proper agreement with spheres of influence recognised. Children are usually delighted by the speed with which a collage picture can be accomplished, especially when it is a combined effort. This gives them no chance to get bored with the project.

Children's ideas for pictures are, more often than not, highly ambitious; unlike adults who recognise their own limitations, children will usually want to produce some epic 'wide-screen' affair. One of the first pictures my eight year old nephew embarked on was the discovery of America by Columbus — and you can't be much more ambitious than that! The picture was never finished. It got slightly bogged down in fact when, in my literal way, I demurred about Columbus planting the Stars and Stripes on virgin soil!

The time to exercise a little discreet guidance is at the beginning when the subject is being chosen. In 'Tree with birds' (fig. 40), Margaret Connor's class of 11-year-olds had a perfect subject in which to combine individuality with co-operation.

Probably the less general scenery you have, the better: landscape, with its necessary perspective, can be very tricky to handle, especially by a group. One child who has been asked to produce a background cow may make one five times as big as the central figure of a farmer being produced by two others together — or the figure may turn out to be so big that it will not fit into the picture without hiding everyone else's efforts. Scale is a funny thing and children, like primitive painters, often seem to see it in terms of importance rather than distance. It isn't necessary, goodness knows, for a child's picture to be flawlessly correct in scale and perspective, but a figure that completely obscures everything else in the picture is a problem. So choose, if possible, a simple, direct subject for group work and have a good working sketch for the team to refer to.

My nephew James, who made 'Goal!' (fig. 41), is an independent person, so when he had drawn his sketch, I helped him choose the materials and then left him to get on with the picture on his own, being in any case quite unqualified to advise on such a subject as football. He has shown a reporter's flair in portraying a scene very familiar to him as an ardent football fan. I believe this shows a fixture when Chelsea played Liverpool and certainly the crowd is fairly evenly matched between those who are grinning

Fig. 40 Tree with Birds, by group of 11-year-old girls
Fig. 41 (*Overleaf*) Goal!, by James Kay, aged 8

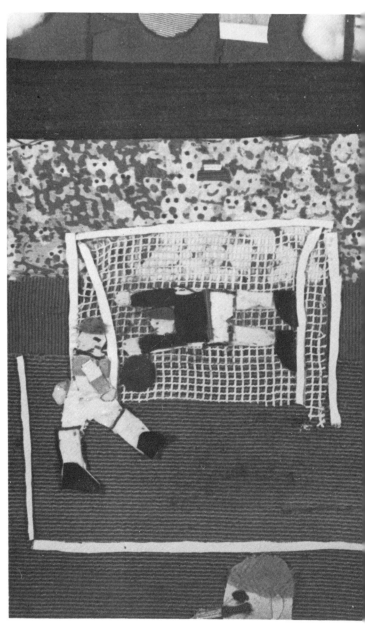

JAMES KAY.

at a home win and those who are looking glum. Keen observation has led to details like the roll of paper being thrown onto the field, the head of the referee, just showing with whistle to mouth, and the wildly athletic goalkeeper just failing to save the goal. I don't suppose this picture would have been possible, if we hadn't managed to find some mottled grey and white material suitable for the crowd. That particular material keeps appearing, as old ruined abbeys, plastered walls, and all kinds of things. I bless the friend who cut a wide strip off the bottom of a skirt to give it to me.

A co-operative effort that turned out in a rather individual way was William Gregory's 'Fish', (fig. 42). William directed operations and his mother did a good deal of the work. I gave occasional assistance too. William selected the subject, chose the materials, drew out the 'blueprint' and did a bit of the general sticking, but on the whole he preferred to delegate the work of interpreting his design.

On the other hand, Andrew, who came to my studio to do his 'Hunting scene' (fig. 43), started by telling me: 'I think you should know that I am a person who doesn't much like to be helped.' I respected this and, if he did invite a bit of help over the hills and hedges, it was only because time was rather pressing. When I offered a suggestion about one of the horses, he very politely told me that he went riding regularly, which he knew very well I didn't. He certainly achieved a convincing picture and, if the seat of the further rider is a little slack like his reins, that explains why horse and rider have fallen a field behind! When the picture was finally finished and pinned to the wall, Andrew and I hugged each other in silent satisfaction. He later wrote to me that he was going to let his grandfather have the picture on 'a long lone' of some weeks.

Fig. 44 was arranged as a combined effort between Derek Nimmo's daughter Amanda and myself. Amanda, who had previously done a collage of her mother sunbathing face-down, did not feel up to portraiture but wanted to do a picture of her father, so we agreed she should do the television set and 'interference' and I would supply the face. We wanted to get the words 'Do not adjust your set' onto the screen, of course, and I rather fancied another line of interference, but I had made Mr Nimmo's face too big to allow anything else to fit onto the screen without obscuring his soulful features. I am afraid this is an object-lesson of the dangers I have been talking about. I was the offender, not Amanda.

Sarah, my niece, declined to do a picture of her doctor father

Fig. 42 Fish, by William Gregory, aged 8, and his mother
Fig. 43 Hunting Scene, by Andrew Cox, aged 9

DO NOT ADJUST YOUR SET.

Fig. 44 Derek Nimmo as the Rev. Mervyn Noote, on TV, by Amanda Nimmo, aged 9, and Frances Kay

Opposite
Fig. 45 Swan Lake, by Sarah Kay, aged 12
Fig. 46 Sweep, by Catherine Armstrong, aged 8

at work, while Amanda was doing hers. Sarah is a romantic and prefers the world of poetry or the theatre to the world of hospitals. She produced 'Swan Lake' (fig. 45). It certainly convinces me that there is familiar music going on as the curtain glides back, and I feel I know just what the slightly bald conductor looks like face to face. We were lucky to find a bit of slightly moulting fur for his head.

Catherine Armstrong who made 'The Sweep' (fig. 46) is another independent person who knows exactly what she wants to do. The daughter of an artist, she knew just how to go to work, with great seriousness. Doing this picture really started her looking at chimneys too. If, through trying a picture, a child starts to learn to look with acute observation at the world around, then the whole project will have been worthwhile. Most of us, as any detective would confirm, go about in blinkers.

Fig. 47 Jack and Jill, by Jennifer Stewart, aged 17

While young children like to portray the excitements of the world around them in a vivid, direct way, as they get older they often veer away from this first-hand directness of vision.

None of the younger children I was working with wanted to portray nursery rhymes, or figures from fiction. It was a sophisticat-

Fig. 48 The Age of Chivalry, by Catharine Potter, aged 16

ed 17-year-old who produced 'Jack and Jill' (fig. 47) and a 16-year-old, well in with all the latest trends, who escaped to mediaeval times with 'The Age of Chivalry' (fig. 48). I wish more people kept their first fresh, direct vision right through adulthood.

Fig. 49 Gluing down the string over the outline of the crown
Fig. 50 Embellishing the gilded crown with 'jewels'
Fig. 51 (*Opposite*) King Henry VIII

Using string

If you have few spare fabrics you are prepared to sacrifice to children, or you just want an occupation to amuse them, you can start them off doing a string collage on either canvas or cardboard. It is rather like a durable form of doodling. This would be the perfect occupation for a wet afternoon in early December, with Christmas cards in mind. You might suggest a very simple outlined Christmas tree or candle or star and, if you are working with very small children, you may like to do the outline with them, drawing it very boldly with a felt pen on white card, as has been done in fig. 49. The child can then glue string to the outline, cutting the string where necessary at junctions. When the glue has dried, the motif—crown, tree, candle, star or whatever you have thought of—can be cut out carefully and sprayed with gold or silver paint. With small children, it is as well to have an adult with plenty of newspaper on hand for this operation, if you do not want to end up with gold or silver children, walls and furniture as well.

Fig. 50 shows the gilded crown being embellished with strings of imitation pearls and flat 'emeralds'. This kind of decoration can be applied to book-marks, book covers, or any of these small objects children like to give at Christmas. Perhaps, more usefully, string could be used to make a set of monograms on canvas, which could be stuck to your luggage to make it more distinctive. A gold, jewelled crown on your luggage might be going too far!

Fig. 52 Camel, by Catherine Armstrong, aged 8
Fig. 53 (*Opposite*) String abstract, by Elizabeth Yauner, Whitelands College

String can be used as simply as in Catherine Armstrong's 'Camel' (fig. 52), or with the sophistication of Elizabeth Yauner's abstract (fig. 53), which is done with three different shades of string and incorporates lentels and other seeds. It makes a very decorative small panel and almost suggests wood inlay. This is the work of an adult, but it shows the kind of design a child could aim at, given string and such common kitchen stores as lentels, dried peas and coffee beans.

An interlacing design, such as appears in some Renaissance pictures, or the kind on Celtic crosses, meticulously carried out in different shades of string, would make an elegant top to a coffee table, under glass. For a richer effect, you could use different coloured cords, including gold cord if you wanted to be really sumptuous. A florentine design in black and gold could be very effective. If you start experimenting, tying decorative knots, fraying out the ends of the string etc, you and the children should find there are infinite possibilities for original designs.

Alternatively you might find string collage useful for stage costumes. A shield or breast-plate in cardboard, decorated with a coat of arms in string or rope, all sprayed gold, would look impressive from the audience.

6 Personal techniques

General advice

As fabric collage is so personal an art, I am going, in this chapter, to give you advice based on the way I do things, and then, in the next chapter, show you the very varied styles and techniques of artists who are masters of their own chosen methods.

I am supposing you are going to embark on a picture a good deal more ambitious than any attempted in chapter 4.

How carefully you sketch your picture first, before committing it to fabric, will probably depend on temperament. Some people, and I am one, feel much more confident with a pair of scissors than a pencil, and therefore do not like to spend long at the drawing board. Others may prefer to draw their picture in some detail, but they must be prepared to adapt it, to suit the materials as they go along, unless they want to end up with a 'painting by numbers' effect.

I would suggest that you start with something not too big. A picture not bigger than 18″ × 15″ would be reasonably easy to handle, not too extravagant with fabric and not too expensive to frame when finished. Or, of course, you may like to work to the size of a frame you already possess.

First decide on your backing. I suggest that unless you feel more at ease working on rigid hardboard, you start with pelmet-weight vilene (pellon), cut rather bigger than the sketch of the finished picture. If you choose hardboard, then carry your background material right over it and lace it across tightly at the back, both from top to bottom and from side to side. With this method, of course, you cannot alter the size of your picture on afterthought.

Collect the materials you think you will need, as though you were squeezing paints onto your palette. If the fabrics 'fight' with each other now, you are doomed from the start!

You will find the various techniques, such as fraying, mounting etc, described beside the picture in which they have been used.

Cat sampler

I did fig. 54 to show how the materials available can, and indeed should, guide your choice of style. The bland cat in the middle, for instance, would not have had the same character if made out of black fur, as it has made out of an old courtelle cardigan, with features taken from the background cotton. The Paiseley cat, (top right) had his shape dictated by the curlings of the paiseley design, and the fierce nature of the Rum Tum Tugger cat (bottom right)

Fig. 54 Cat sampler (Courtesy Mrs. Z. Murray)

was suggested by the lines of the black and white cotton cut from the hem of a dress. Of the others, the alley cat (top left) is black velvet, the home cat (top centre) is black and white artificial fur, the Pop cat is 'pop' floral material rearranged, the small mouse occupying a vacant site near the middle is brown suede, the Top Cat (centre right) is painted velvet, and the kitten with mother is rabbit fur.

53

A picture of the sampler kind eliminates the need to glue on any large expanse of material for background. Sticking background fabric to the backing is often the trickiest process of the whole picture. Work from top to bottom (or bottom to top), spreading the glue in bands across, then anchor the materials together with a paperweight while you go on to spread the next band. It is usually better to spread the glue onto the fabric, not the backing, as the backing, especially vilene (pellon), is likely to absorb too much glue. Most rubber-adhesive glues, like Copydex, Sobo, or Elmers keep their powers of adhesion while they are drying, so there is no need to work in haste. It is misleading to iron some fabrics onto backing, as the heat of the iron may shrink the fabric in relation to the backing so that as they cool down blisters begin to appear where the surface had seemed flat. If you have a background such as a wide expanse of sky, it may prove necessary, in the last resort, to introduce a few clouds or birds over any air blisters or obtrusive glue.

Flower piece

In fig. 55 I used black felt for the upper background and green rayon tweed for the lower: both very easy fabrics to deal with. I usually like to portray realistic flowers like roses, peonies and lilies, which lend themselves particularly well to fabric collage, but on this occasion I had some stylised materials in purples, scarlet, flame and lime green that I wanted to use. So I turned my back on my usual source of inspiration, the old Dutch masters, and the initial inspiration for this picture, although it scarcely shows it, was a Persian carpet. Having been inspired by the flowing design of flowers entwined with birds, writhing out of an oriental vase, I let my own materials dictate the way the picture should go. I made a very rough sketch which indicated the general shape of the vase and the arrangement flowing out of it, but no more than a general indication.

As I had a piece of coarse écru lace, I decided to use that, mounted on coffee-coloured repp (transversely corded fabric), to make the vase. Handles were made from some other large-scale écru-coloured lace edging, cut and pieced together to make the shapes I wanted. I usually contain the flowers in a wide-necked vase, urn or basket, using lace over cotton for vases and interwoven braid for baskets. Sometimes, inspired by Dutch pictures, I put in a bird's nest made of ends of wool and fabric, containing a few pale blue cotton eggs. Often a beetle or caterpillar creeps

Fig. 55 Flower piece

up to the vase too, but in this stylised piece I kept insect life down to a minimum and only put in one butterfly where there was a gap in the design.

Each flower is made separately as an entity. For this picture, I first made all the flower stems. I like stems to be pliable and rounded, so I use piping cord covered with strips of bias-cut material: in this case, all lime green, to unify the picture. I knew from my sketch roughly how many large and how many smaller flowers I needed. I made up the flower heads (blossoms) on small bases of vilene (pellon), combining petals gathered from different stylised designs that seemed to blend in shape and colour. These blossoms were then glued to lengths of stem that I knew could be shortened as needed. When I had prepared a number of flowers, I started to lay them with their stems going into the vase, as though it were a real arrangement. At this stage, nothing was glued. I started with the outer flowers and worked towards the middle, keeping an important flower for the focal centre. The leaves can be stuck onto the stems just where they are needed, at a later stage – something you cannot do with real flowers. But just as in a real arrangement, the colours have to be carefully blended. The birds were made up separately on vilene (pellon), with legs of russian braid. The birds had to be more carefully pre-designed than the flowers to get the balance right. When sticking the flowers and stems down, one has to have a clear picture in mind of which flowers are meant to come forward, which to recede, so that the stems are stuck down behind or in front of flowers with a consistent relationship of depth. A flower picture is considered by many people one of the most congenial kinds of picture to have about the house.

Fig. 56 The Awfulness of Feeling Overdressed

Garden picture

Although also concerned with plants, the problems in the garden picture (fig. 56) were quite different from the flower arrangement. Here I wanted to blend the different greens to give an impression of natural growth and to give depth to the whole picture with black net shadows. The juxtaposing of different fabrics is of great importance in a picture like this: each gains from contrast with the neighbouring materials. I was lucky enough to have a piece of guipure lace of the right design and scale for the garden seat and some pale moiré for the marble statues. These set off the flowing growth of the plants by contrast. I have used a fraying-out technique for trees, shrubs, plants and ferns. After cutting out the material in the shape of natural growth, the edge is deliberately frayed to variable depth. Interesting effects can be achieved, especially where the fabric is shot. Three different shades of green, cut in feather-shaped branches, were laid over each other, showing the feathery tips, to make the shrub on centre right. The ferns in the foreground were made by cutting pale green repp to fern shapes and then fraying out the edges, leaving just a few warp threads down each centre to hold the 'fern' together. These were given a centre vein of narrow cord. All the other plants use variations of fraying, with the addition of raffia, net, lace (dyed green) and a few lighter green threads overlaying the branches of the cedar tree (top right).

The gnome, separately made up on vilene (pellon), was the germinating point of the whole picture, but a lot of people have said they would prefer it without him. As one of the advantages of collages is that they can be changed, I will probably supply a separate peacock (and title) to replace the gnome if so desired!

Sea picture

As I have already indicated, nature likes things frayed at the edges: think of grass, clouds, feathers and spray as well as branches; so that despite many people's concern about the problems of fraying it can be shown to be a positive asset. Fig. 57 employs a good deal of deliberate fraying, to get the effect of blown spume. Bunched white raffia has also been used for the crests of the waves.

Fig. 57 (*Overleaf*) Rough Sea

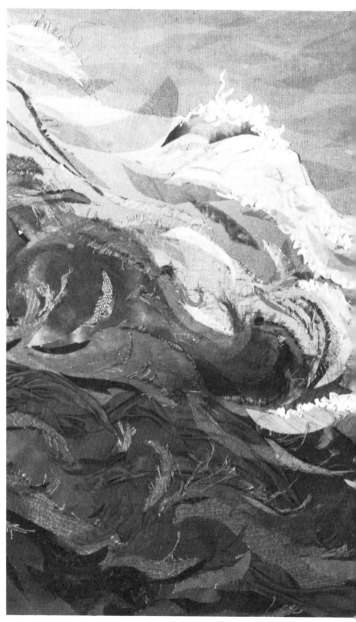

If you particularly do not want the fabric to fray because, for instance, you want to cut a crenellated edge for a castle, you can either press it onto self-adhesive vilene (pellon), or glue it to some cotton, such as an old sheet. Two materials stuck together should not fray. You can then cut out the crenellations, or other features, through the two materials stuck together, and apply them to the picture. To give a feature extra 'body', it sometimes proves very useful to glue it onto a thick material, such as felt, before applying it. Had I wanted to insert a seagull riding the waves in this picture, I would have mounted my cotton onto felt, so that it would not have been lost in the folds of the waves.

I am often asked: how do you stop the glue coming through? This can be tricky. The makers of Copydex say you should spread it very thinly on both surfaces to be stuck and leave to dry before applying them together. But sometimes, even with this care, glue will come through thin silk in an absolutely sickening way. One answer is to use thin materials only when bunched, folded or swathed. In fig. 57 some of the waves have been formed by swathes of fine silk. By this method all traces of glue can be hidden in the folds.

River picture

Fig. 58 is an atmospheric sort of picture. I have always loved the Thames at night, with strings of light along the Embankment and a slight mist over the water. This picture depends almost entirely on having the appropriate materials and deploying them correctly. As this is a nocturne, all the fabrics are in tones of black, through grey to silver on the water, with just a point of pale gold for the electric light bulb and an echo of gold in the light it sheds.

The dark grey moiré silk for the sky was applied first, then the furthest group of factory building and skyscraper; the factory, made of fine black grosgrain, and the skyscraper were then covered with two layers of grey net. The same grosgrain, covered in one layer of grey net, made the centre group of industrial buildings and, with braids and ribbon applied and unobscured by net, it also made the nearest building, Lots Road Power Station. But before gluing on the middle and near buildings, the silver-grey rayon was applied for the river. Next the barges and their buoys were put on. Then black, grey and white net were blended in over the rayon to make the shadows and ripples of the river. I know some people say that you cannot satisfactorily apply net without stitching it. I think you can. Try putting the glue on lightly with a

Fig. 58 Chelsea Embankment (Courtesy Patrick Helmore)

finger, spreading it so that none of the holes are clogged when it
is applied. If you then anchor it with a paperweight while it is
adhering, it should stay put. The same applies to cotton wool
(absorbent cotton) for clouds or smoke: not too much glue, and
firm anchorage while it is sticking.

The parapet depends for its solidity on the weave of the different
materials going in the right directions: diagonally for the rayon
going along on top of the river wall and vertically for the black

corduroy that forms the wall itself. Lastly the ornately moulded lamp standards, with perspective not forgotten, were made up outside the picture, the braids being taken round to the back of the corduroy to give a solid effect. The viewpoint of this picture, incidentally, is just near where Whistler lived.

Figures

There are of course many ways of making figures in collage, as a glance at the next chapter will show. Here I will describe my own way, a method which precludes the fluidity of say, Vera Sherman's figures (fig. 76), or the impressionism of Ella Raayoni's (fig. 82), but is highly suitable for the beginner, as the figure is made up separately and only committed to the picture when you are satisfied with it. In this way the whole picture will not be wrecked if the figure is not a success. By using vilene (pellon) on which to build up separate units of a picture, I join the 'hard edge' school of collage. For instance, in the train of the frontispiece, each coach was made up separately, and the passengers could then be made and stuck in their places in the coaches, instead of having to be stuck on the background where I hoped the windows of the coach would be. This method has obvious advantages for group work too.

For a figure like Queen Elizabeth I (fig. 59), there is no need to draw in detail onto the vilene (pellon), but it helps to have a fairly accurate outline. After cutting this out, you must always start by applying the material for flesh, where it is going to be exposed. I use a flesh-coloured glazed chintz as a rule, but of course 'flesh-coloured' covers a wide range from Nubian black to anaemic white. I have a range of shades. I can paint in the features on this chintz in some detail, using watercolour paints and a fine brush. Any facial hair (as in Henry VIII, fig. 51) is then applied, using wool or embroidery thread according to the texture wanted. I always enjoy the very hirsute faces most, which is one reason, among many, why scenes from the Old Testament are such a joy to do.

You may prefer to dress your figures first, before putting their faces on. It is not unlike dressing a doll, and the glue should not be too liberally applied, so that there is a suggestion of freedom in the clothes.

Full skirts should be taken round to the back, so that no hint of a raw edge is ever left at the side. By this method, arms and legs can often be attached quite separately to find the most

Fig. 59 Queen Elizabeth I

natural position. As I say, this method may be considered by some to be primitive, but nobody could deny that it is fun to do.

One word of warning from bitter experience: before embarking on your figure in detail, make sure where in the picture it is to be placed, so that it is not too ridiculously big or small in relation to the things around it, nor, after much trouble over it, is it found to be half obscured by a horse or a courtier. That sort of thing can be very upsetting.

Making a picture with a figure in it: The Master Mariner

Fig. 60 Rough sketch of the picture, showing the general placing of figure in relation to deck etc.

Fig. 61 Collection of all the materials used.

Fig. 62 Shaded blue sateen for the sky being stuck to the base vilene, with the palest part where the horizon will be.

Fig. 63 A small scrap of blue and green jaspé cotton for the sea being stuck down at a slight tilt, to indicate swell.

Fig. 64 Brown moiré for the deck has been applied, overlapping the sky and sea fabrics, and all are being trimmed from the back.

Fig. 65 Deck furnishings have been added. Striped material makes a beer barrel, a coil of rope is made from piping cord, russian braid is used for rigging, white PVC (vinyl) for the deck rail, and white piqué for the seagull, with a bead for an eye. The setting is now complete.

Fig. 66 Cutting out the figure in vilene (pellon). Where the hand overlaps the knee, the hand is cut out. This shows clearly in fig. 69.

Fig. 67 Applying flesh coloured cotton over face and arms.

Fig. 68 Trimming the flesh material from the back.

Fig. 69 Trimming dark blue cotton which has been applied for trousers.

Fig. 70 Trimming red and white striped shirt, with pale blue front already inset.

Fig. 71 This shows how the shirt is stuck on, bringing the fabric round to the back for greater reality.

Fig. 72 Belt and shoes of black PVC (vinyl) have been applied and decorated with motifs cut from silver lace. A white piqué collar and rolled up sleeves, cut on the bias, have been added. Black embroidery thread is being applied to make the hair.

Fig. 73 All the hair has been added and the ribboned hat put over it. The hand is being cut to hold the long pipe made of PVC (vinyl).

Fig. 74 The eyes, nose, mouth and a suitable tattoo have been painted in with watercolours. The Master Mariner is now stuck in position.

Fig. 60

Fig. 61   Fig. 62

Fig. 63   Fig. 64

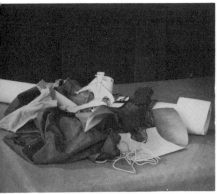

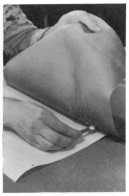

Fig. 65

Fig. 66   Fig. 67

Fig. 68   Fig. 69

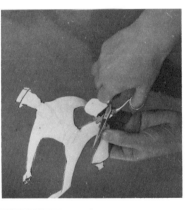

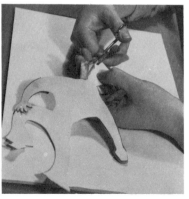

Fig. 70   Fig. 71

Fig. 72

Fig. 73   Fig. 74

7 Other artists' techniques

Style

I think it could be said of collage that, to an even greater extent than in painting, style and technique are interdependent.

You may well be feeling that you want to break right away from the degree of realism I have shown in my own work. There is a tremendous enthusiasm for 'free design' abroad in the world, unfettered by any connection with representation or even with symbolism—and this is indeed liberating. But it has its dangers. Free design, unfettered by any discipline at all, is just a mess. Embroidery, because it imposes its own strict disciplines of technique, is probably a more profitable medium than collage for free design. Collage must be harnessed to a consistent style and technique, whatever you are expressing in your picture, whether it is an abstract of a type that might be titled 'Illusion', or a study of a rose.

In this chapter I shall introduce you to a range of artists who have mastered their very different styles. Each one seems to tackle the challenge of so much scope quite individually and to develop his particular gifts for colour, pattern, narrative, atmosphere, or even social comment.

It is, perhaps, rash to generalise about technique, but I think possibly collagists can be grouped into those who practise a 'hard edge' technique and those whose style and technique are fluid. There are particular virtues in both; the 'hard edge' pictures can have a three dimensional quality and impact peculiar to this medium. The 'fluid' pictures have movement and the imaginative quality of impressionist paintings.

Successful collagists do not always keep to the same style. Margaret Kaye's work has become more and more fluid with the years, as she seems to be ever more intent on expressing the inner essence, rather than the outer form, of each subject she tackles. She has all along been a path-finder in collage and others have followed where she has led the way.

Fig. 75 (*Opposite*) Figures, by Margaret Kaye

70

Anyone who is still wondering what fabric collage is all about would do well to study closely fig. 76. This portrayal of 'Rush Hour' could not have been achieved with its marvellous sense of movement in any other medium but fabric collage. Paint could not have captured the interplay of lustre and texture; embroidery, by the deliberation of stitching, must have arrested the flow of line. Here the sense of urgent movement is caught precisely, but without the subject being nailed down in anything like a representational way.

This is collage at its most fluid. Vera Sherman specialises in movement. It is the leit-motif in all her bird and figure studies. Her 'Fighting Cock' (fig. 7, page 15) shows this momentum, and it is apparent whether she is portraying a wheeling flock of gulls, or a strutting turkey-cock. Instead of moving from subject to subject, she has made a concentrated study of birds—and now of figures. (The connection between the movement of a fighting cock and a commuter may, or may not, be accidental.) Her concentration makes for a unity of style, and most people who have studied fabric collage could recognise a Vera Sherman picture, without having to see the V.S. signature on it.

Let no-one imagine that, to capture this effect of flowing movement, all you need to do is to tear your fabrics into careless shapes, fray out the edges a bit, and then stick them down on to your backing with impulsive abandon. Speaking from experience, I can say that this artless lack of technique is likely to call forth the comment: 'Oh', (long pause) 'what happened to that one?' You need to have a very clear idea in your mind, before you start, of the effect you are aiming for. Be prepared to experiment at length with pieces pinned on, with the background at a vertical angle, and collect a wide range of lustrous silks, velvets, lurex etc to use in contrast to matt linens and canvas, which act as the foil to your highlight materials.

Vera Sherman has arranged some exciting exhibitions of fabric pictures in a wide range of style from the fluid work of Margaret Kaye and herself to the incisive template technique of Eirian Short.

Fig. 76 (*Opposite*) Rush Hour, by Vera Sherman (Courtesy Reading Education Committee)

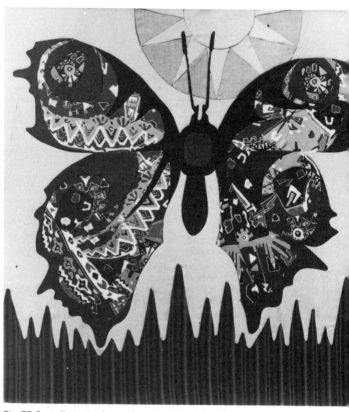

Fig. 77 Butterfly in the Grass (54" × 54"), by Eirian Short

Template technique

Eirian Short has studied sculpture in the past and now teaches design at an art college, as well as having written on fabric collage and embroidery. Among the varied techniques she uses and teaches, she has evolved one in which she cuts out her designs in hardboard with a jig-saw. The pieces are then covered in fabric, re-assembled, and stuck with Evo-stick (Elmer's or Sobo in U.S.) on to a hardboard backing. 'Butterfly in the grass' is a deftly clear example of this method. The fabric which makes all the butterfly markings was the original inspiration for this picture. As you can imagine, this method calls for great precision. In skilled hands it makes a strong impact. It is very suitable for anybody who wants to try out geometrical designs, especially of the

Fig. 78 Felt Inlay (36″ × 48″), by Robert Preston, Hornsey College of Art

kind known as 'op' art. Imagine a design showing two 'targets' side by side, each with a series of roundels in shades from pink to red; in one the roundels would be piled on each other with the deepest red in the centre, in the other the gradation would go the other way, with the palest pink in the centre, the deepest red on the outside. I think it would make an interesting effect.

A variation on the template technique is 'Felt inlay', (fig. 78) by Robert Preston. Here the felt is cut to fit exactly piece into piece and glued on to hardboard. You would need to equip your-self with a pair of compasses and a ruler for this kind of work and you would have to work with the precision of an architect. Thus smoothly worked, particularly on a grand scale as it is here, this kind of picture is most impressive. If there were gaps at the joints, they would show up as an obvious failure.

Fig. 79 Cool Landscape, by Helen Hutton

Fumage, brulage and décollage techniques

In complete contrast to the work of the four artists already mentioned is that of Helen Hutton, helping to prove the wide range of style covered by fabric collage.

'Cool Landscape' (fig. 79) is a highly sophisticated picture, evoking ideas of moon scenery. To achieve this evocative picture the artist has used the techniques of fumage (smoking the fabric), brulage (burning holes in it), and décollage (tearing away parts of the fabric). She uses Japanese rag paper, cotton rag, and tissue paper, torn or singed but never cut. On a primed or painted hardboard backing, reinforced with wood battens to stop it warping while damp, she uses a wallpaper paste, such as Polycel, and on to this applies ruckled rag paper and cotton, smoking them and sometimes burning holes to get the effects she wants. She dampens the rag to get more control over the area to be treated — and she has a bucket of water handy. Finally her pictures may be varnished with a polyurethane plastic coating, such as Polyglaze. This method, which may sound like a lark, probably needs more mental discipline than any other.

Fig. 80 The Fountain, Witley Court, by Angela Steveni (Courtesy Dr. E. Harrold)

Impressionism

I think Angela Steveni's work, almost more than any other, needs to be seen in fabric rather than reproduced by photography. However clever the photographer, her subtleties of colour, tone and texture elude the photographic plate. In fig. 80 she has done a haunting picture of a haunting ruin. Layers of transparent fabric are laid one over the other in subtle gradations of colour, to produce an ethereal effect impossible in any other medium. Machine stitching has been used quite a lot here, but essentially it is a collage.

For this kind of picture you need a confident technique but, more than that, an artist's eye and a poet's mind. Personally, I find a strange alchemy at work in her pictures, so that the total impact is about six times as great as the sum of the parts out of which they are created.

The work of 'Beldy' (Mrs Mabel Maugham) is also ethereal in a very personal style. Some of her pictures seem to be blown together and to stay put by magic, so little evidence is there of stitching or glue. Her technique is her own secret—and I don't

Fig. 81 Roses, by 'Beldy' (Courtesy Victoria and Albert Museum)

suppose anybody else could achieve pictures like hers, even given the exact know-how. It is almost impossible not to write in terms of butterfly's wings, so diaphanous are her effects. 'Roses' (fig. 81) is an early work, very subtle in colouring, particularly with all the gradations of white. She has exhibited in Boston, New York and London, as well as in Italy, France and Switzerland. Anyone wanting to emulate her work would need a huge range of subtly tinted gauzy fabrics as well as an impressionist's eye and a gossamer touch.

Impressionist in style, but completely individual in technique, is the work of Ella Raayoni, an Israeli artist. She has a uniquely free way of sketching in effects with a single thread, thus catching forms with great delicacy. It is all done by pure collage, no stitching being used.

In 'Mosque at Acre' (fig. 82) she manages to evoke the feel of the Eastern Mediterranean. Her subject matter is very varied—figures, landscape, flowers—but her style is so individual that her work is unmistakable.

Sometimes her pictures suggest Matisse, but the particular effects she achieves could only have been caught in fabric. However, the work of Matisse would make a profitable subject for study for anyone tackling fabric collage. His command of rhythmic patterns in juxtaposition could provide a helpful guide to composition, especially remembering that he took up collage himself in his old age.

If you can master Ella Raayoni's technique of 'sketching' with a thread or two, you will have new territories of collage to explore. Portraiture comes to mind, and architectural studies.

Fig. 82 Mosque at Acre, by Ella Raayoni (Courtesy Heal's London)

Further techniques

'Gateway to Atlantis' (fig. 83) and also 'Master Race' (fig. 24, page 27) are by Mary Ffrench, a self-taught artist who has evolved a distinctive style of her own. She started fabric collage only four years ago, having done a good deal of dress-making and some amateur stage work which is evident in some of the theatrical effects she achieves. Working with a stage designer would probably be helpful for every collagist.

Mary Ffrench has the great benefit of a very co-operative husband who makes her frames and acts as an honest but appreciative critic. Her first attempt at a collage picture kept her at work for a whole weekend, cutting and gluing. The result was a picture of a fish agonisingly struggling to get out of a fishing net. It is an uncomfortable and powerful picture. Her husband looked at it for a while in silence and then said: 'Well, I don't really like it, but you must certainly go on!' And she has gone on from strength to strength.

Her subject matter is very varied and her pictures often include bits of theatrical odds and ends and even the odd creature, such as the real sea-horses and star fishes disporting themselves in the sea-weed at the Atlantis gateway in fig. 83.

One of her individual techniques is to machine-embroider separately on to vilene (pellon) some central feature of her picture, encrusting it with textural interest, and then stick it to the picture with glue. The tree form under the boot in fig. 24 has been treated in this manner. This can be a very effective way of mixing machine embroidery with collage and it shows how anyone, working independently, can make his own innovations and so enrich the scope of his work. Mary Ffrench is constantly experimenting with different methods, subject matter and materials. If I wanted to commission a series of fairy story illustrations in fabric collage, she is the artist I would choose to do them. She has both the imagination and the technique to portray dragons laying waste the land, and sugar-plum fairies.

Margaret Connor's work is based on very true observation. She inspires the young pupils she teaches with her own enthusiasm and, through lecturing and exhibiting, she has fired many people with an interest in fabric collage who had never heard of it before.

She lives in the north of England and her work is very much rooted in that part of the country, whether she is doing a pastoral or an industrial scene, as I mentioned in the chapter on Sources of Inspiration. A picture like 'The Beach' (fig. 84) may look simple,

Fig. 83 Gateway to Atlantis, by Mary Ffrench

Fig. 84 The Beach, by Margaret Connor (Courtesy Mrs Breton, Pudsey)

and great fun to do, but its success is based on its true portrayal of tones in the receding headlands and the overshadowing rocks in the right foreground. The objets trouvés (found objects) she has used have been applied with discipline and not just flung wholesale over the shore. This type of picture may look deceptively simple and spontaneous, but I know from experience that it needs great precision and a well-stocked cupboard of fabrics and bits and pieces. It is also the kind of picture for which a coloured photograph may well have proved an inspiration in the first place, but it would have been a disaster if the photograph had been too slavishly imitated.

Georgina Hammick's innocent 'Country Scene' (fig. 85) is another that may look insouciant, but in fact it is worked out with great skill by someone who has studied art in Paris and in England and knows exactly what to aim for. The shapes of the cows, the net ripples on the river water, the blossoming tree are all entertainingly making the most of the fabric medium. The simpler the

Fig. 85 Country Scene, by Georgina Hammick

picture, the better the draftsmanship needs to be—and this is not a bad rule to keep in mind.

The lyrical essence of a pastoral scene like this seems to me more exactly conveyed in velvets, net and felt, than it could be in watercolours by any but a master's hand. Freshness of vision and touch have a lot to do with it.

Many art critics are not inclined to take fabric collage seriously as a medium, but they do not lightly dismiss the work of Margaret Kaye. Through all her work, in the twenty years or so that she has been making pictures with fabric, the unmistakable quality of a serious artist has been obvious. She has happened to find the texture of fabric a sympathetic medium to work with, but there is nothing of 'the handy little needlewoman' about her bold approach. She has blazed a trail, gained recognition in the art jungle where dealers prowl and now, through teaching at art colleges and through her one-man exhibitions, she has gained many disciples.

Fig. 86 Bull with Pigeons, by Margaret Kaye (Courtesy Victoria and Albert Museum)

The two pictures of hers shown here are an early work, 'Bull with Pigeons', and a recent one, 'Bison' (figs. 86 and 87). There is a good deal of stitchery on the early work, while the later one is pure collage. Both portray the essence of bovine strength, that massive shouldered thrust of weight that epitomises both animals. But apart from their study in strength, the sheer decorative quality of these two pictures is remarkable. Anyone who could enter a room containing a picture by Margaret Kaye without being struck by it, would have to be blind indeed.

I think the lessons that a collage beginner can most easily learn from studying reproductions of Margaret Kaye's work, are spiritual rather than technical. To be as free with the medium as she now is demands years of experience. But her courage in blaz-

82

Fig. 87 Bison, by Margaret Kaye

ing her own trail and for ever questing and experimenting, without ever becoming dogmatic, are qualities that every collagist should try to emulate.

Another exciting experimenter and innovator is Eugenie Alexander, one of the most successful and versatile collagists working today. She began, at a very early age, experimenting with a collage of marmalade, mixed with dye, on wallpaper, and went on with many other experiments in more orthodox media before discovering that it was fabric she really wanted to work with. All the experience she gained in practising textile design, lithography, modelling and painting, has given her work in fabric a specially confident authority.

Fig. 88 Blue Monkey, (42" × 50"), by Eugenie Alexander
Fig. 89 (*Opposite*) Tuba Player, by Frank Johnson (Courtesy General Trading Company, London)

She uses some stitching, both by machine and hand, on her collages, her range is wide and her use of colour is bold, but most noticeable is the variety of mood in her work, from the lyrical dreaminess of 'Cliffside' (fig. 13, page 16) to the arresting ferocity of 'Blue Monkey' (fig. 88).

Sometimes, as in 'Eve and the Tiger' (fig. 90), her pictures remind one of the work of Le Douanier Rousseau and she has a real flair for portraying jungles which, as I have already indicated, need tremendous control to be convincing in collage. To get her effects, she is prepared to study her subject for hours, to arrange and re-arrange her materials pinned to the background — and then to be ready to alter a whole picture radically, if she is not satisfied with it. This professional dedication produces pictures that have a spontaneous gaiety.

Eugenie Alexander has also had very successful exhibitions of her work, and has written a delightful book on fabric pictures in both collage and embroidery (see page 102).

Frank Johnson is another artist whose pictures appear effortlessly gay but are, in fact, the product of a very professional approach. His 'Tuba player' (fig. 89) was included, although there is a lot of stitching in it, because it shows so well the humorous possibilities of collage—a deft touch of caricature in the figure, a Ruritanian lavishness of decoration, and one can almost hear Souza coming out of the tuba. Many of his pictures show unmistakable figures from history, such as Abraham Lincoln and George V. This approach may open up a wide field of possibilities to the beginner in collage. Good draftsmanship will be your most necessary ability—and a good eye for colour. Given these, the Daughters of the American Revolution, the mayors of remote boroughs, the cheer-leaders of college campuses and the Yeomen of the Guard may all be captured in fabric to make colourful decorations.

In a rather different genre, Charles Hammick's work reflects pomp and pageantry. He also is a complete professional, paying fastidious attention to detail. Fig. 91 is both an elegant design and a faithful rendering of historic costume.

I hope the enormously wide variety of work shown in this chapter has convinced you that the scope of fabric collage is tremendous. In spite of the differences in all these artists' styles and the huge field that they cover, there is still room, I feel sure, for new artists working in completely individual ways; and these examples may encourage you to experiment and so discover a personal style and technique of your own.

Fig. 90 (*Opposite*) Eve and the Tiger, by Eugenie Alexander
Fig. 91 (*Opposite*) Officer of the 7th Hussars *c.*1835, by Charles Hammick

8 Abstract pictures

At present art colleges are turning out very much more abstract than figurative collage work. They use colour with a great outburst of confident liberation and they design with panache, so that the often gaunt corridors of the new colleges are splashed with brilliant designs. They have sumptuous resources of textiles to draw on, no inhibitions about mixing materials, and inspired teachers to guide them and impose the necessary degree of discipline into their work. Lucky students; lucky everyone who has a bag of fabrics, a tube of glue, and imagination.

Abstract and figurative artists sometimes mistrust each other's integrity, because the stresses are so different. Collage would be much less interesting if there were not scope for both approaches, and I think most people would benefit by trying both: who knows what latent talent may be dormant in somebody struggling to make an exactly faithful reproduction of a tree out of green tweed? You should give yourself the chance to get right away from trying to be a camera, and become a kaleidoscope. 'Kaleidoscope' comes from the Greek 'kalos'—beautiful and 'eidos'—form; what better aim for abstract fabric collage?

Fig. 92 Piece of driftwood

Fig. 93 Abstract from fig. 92, by Caroline Beevers (aged 14), Sydenham Comprehensive School

There must be many people who would like to try an abstract picture, but don't quite know where to begin. There are few better places than beside the sea. A walk along the sea shore will probably reveal a dozen ideas. Water is a natural sculptor, moulding the sand and gradually chiselling away at driftwood and rock to leave shapes of great beauty and refinement. Fig. 92 shows a rather beautiful piece of oyster-coloured driftwood, which inspired 14-year-old Caroline Beevers to do the abstract in muted greys, browns, black and white on a natural ground shown in fig. 93. She has succeeded in conveying the restrained subtlety of the wood, which at her age is remarkable. Its flowing lines might also be conveyed in ruffled ribbon, raffia or thick wools.

I would strongly recommend a close study of water-sculpted forms; both their shapes and their subtle colours can provide an enormous variety of ideas.

A number of artists graduate to abstract pictures through figurative; a few vice versa. The first 'progression' is probably the easier to understand. Usually it is a matter of shedding details and concentrating on the essential elements of the subject chosen, until only the skeleton of the original idea remains. People often suspect abstract work, because the terms of reference are not clear. I think if they could see some of the sketch books that have led the way to difficult abstractions, they would have more respect for the uphill process of creativity. Anyone who has watched a film of Picasso at work will have experienced the revelation of seeing the creative mind in the act of creating. Retrospective exhibitions of abstract artists can give one this insight too.

Supposing you become fascinated by the varying play of light on a shot fabric and decide to make an abstract collage to feature this, you may spend hours arranging and rearranging fabric shapes in wheels, spirals or rays to get the maximum variety. Or you may be intrigued by three dimensional possibilities. If the picture is to be safely protected from dust, behind glass, you can experiment with a kind of sculpture in fabric: treating stuffs like the earth's surface in eruption, piled up, fissured, striated and dissolving into mists of gauze. The possibilities are olympian.

A trained artist like Mary Youles can make geometric abstraction fascinating. 'Skittle Alley' (fig. 94), in a range of pink and red shades of ribbon, wool and plastic is a brilliant study in depth, achieved on a flat surface. Every bar seems to have been given exactly the right proportion and position to gain the effect of recession with a feeling of inevitability.

The cool geometric line may well be your starting point, particularly if you live in a 'cool' geometric house. Checked and striped materials, together with ribbons, can produce the kind of picture which gives an illusion of depth, or of absolute solidity. It could be an extension of the kind of illusion our grandmothers played with when they made 'boxes' out of fabrics in patchwork quilts. This kind of design is known to make mathematicians lyrical, provided the equations are correct.

If a mathematical approach to abstraction does not appeal to you, you might one day save your fabric cuttings from another picture and try a more arbitrary approach. Play about with these shapes, arranging and cutting or tearing them, until you are satisfied that they form some sort of balance. If they fall into a really compelling design, sieze it, by sticking the pieces down in place onto card or canvas. This kind of doodling with materials

Fig. 94 Skittle Alley, by Mary Youles (Courtesy Somerset Education Committee)

is never a waste of time if it helps you to discover what makes for balance and cohesion in a picture.

The next time you doodle through a long telephone call, keep your doodle and let it form the springboard for a design. As in figurative types of collage, it probably won't help to draw out your design too carefully first—unless you are doing a purely linear design, in which case you could draw the lines onto the background with a felt pen and then cover them with a variety of matt or glittering ribbons, wools and threads to make your tracery.

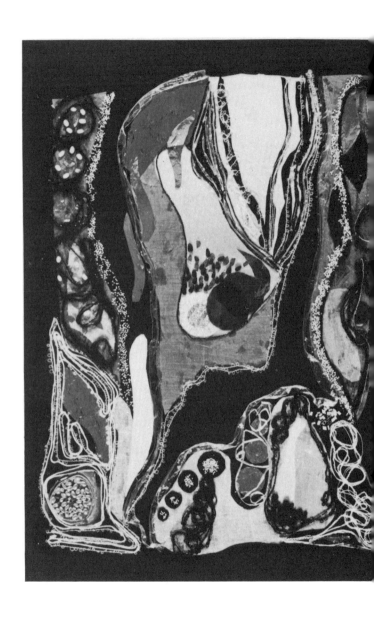

Fig. 95 Pine bark abstract, by Anne Sleeman, Whitelands College

I have even seen a linear abstraction carried out in corset bones and safety pins.

Trees have been a source of inspiration to poets and artists since our ancestors swung about in them. Every part of a tree from its writhing trunk, through the tracery of its branches and leaves, to blossom and fruit suggests pattern and colour.

The glittering abstraction done by Anne Sleeman (fig. 95) was derived from the bark of a pine tree. First she took a rubbing from the bark of the trunk, using soft pencil and pliable paper, then she enlarged the most interesting section of the rubbing, and from the enlargement made her design in silver, white and black, on black card.

The sheer decorative possibilities of abstract collage are tremendous. Think of hanging a collage of ten different tones and textures of black on a pure white wall; or even better, ten different kinds of white on a black wall. White has infinite gradations, from the limpid life of pearly white to the arctic-freeze of blue-whites, from white velvet to crystal silk, to broderie anglaise, to very old off-white lace, to your grandmother's wedding dress, to a string of pearls, to a seagull's feather, to the chalk-white of a broiler egg — all far away from the whiter-than-whiteness of detergent advertisements. If white does excite you, you might find shape for your inspiration in clouds, sheep's fleece, waterfalls, frost crystals or daisies.

Some of your best abstract ideas may occur to you in the bath, as you contemplate the vortex of your disappearing bath water, or the dispersal of steam, or the patterns of bath oil as it spreads through the water.

Another idea, perhaps for commuters or town dwellers who have to use public transport or get stuck in traffic jams in their own cars, is to think of the map of their city as a design. You could either begin this design with a real map, copying the main roads in ribbon, the subways in black braid, the fly-overs (overpasses) in silver, and decorating the parks in some particularly attractive green material and the rivers in blue chiffon over green satin; or you could simply develop an abstract pattern from the over-all shape of the map. A design based on New York would look more balanced than one based on London.

You need never be afraid of somebody else pirating your idea and making your picture in collage. Even if everybody decided to make a design of the same traffic snarl-up, I doubt if any two pictures would turn out to be remotely alike.

Fig. 96 Pomegranate bisected
Fig. 97 (*Opposite*) Pomegranate abstract, by Irene Cooper, Whitelands College
Fig. 98 (*Opposite*) Pomegranate abstract, by Sheila Macintyre, Whitelands College

Fig. 96 shows a bisected pomegranate. To illustrate how differently people interpret things, here are what Irene Cooper and Sheila Macintyre made of it, given the same subject and the same scarlet repp (transversely corded fabric) background (figs. 97 and 98). Both designs are enchantingly gay and inventive: one with its use of fine gold net and exuberant squiggles, the other using melon seeds, lentels etc. Both are worlds away from the stereotyped ecclesiastical pomegranate I can remember having to embroider, taking days to do it and loathing every symbolically fertile little seed I had to satin-stitch. Fertility of design is more often found in the spontaneous, free kind of work done by these two students than in a laborious set piece.

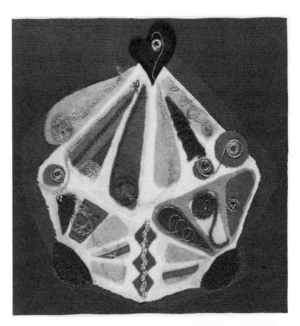

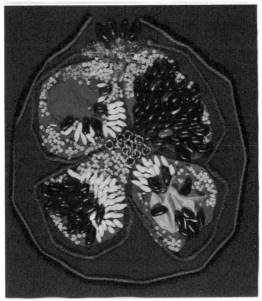

Fig. 99 Abstract, by Daphne Todd, Whitelands College

You may, of course, prefer a shout, rather than a murmur, of colour and choose to express it as an abstract. You might well begin by collecting together all your fabrics in tones of coral through red to purple, and then see what they suggest. It might be the regal pomp of crowns, or the ecclesiastical pomp of mitres, or they might suggest a molten furnace. You might even associate them with something anatomical; it is conceivable that a very beautiful design could be based on the intestines.

96

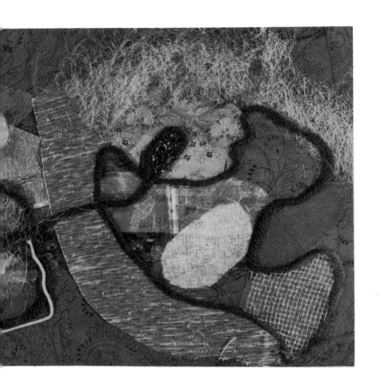

You could start your picture simply by deciding that your room needs a blue-green composition on the wall. Then, according to your taste, you might be inspired by the forms of insects' wings, or oceanic depths, or the spikes of sea holly, or Persian minarets. All these ideas could provide the starting points from which you would extract the essence of shape and texture to produce your final design.

The abstract in orange, reds and purples (fig. 99) was made by a mature student whose first abstract collage this was. I have no idea what was in her mind when she made it but to me it suggests Release.

9 Finishing, framing and hanging

Finishing

I would like to dedicate this chapter to my patient framer: the man who has to remove whiskers of material clinging uninvited to the face of the picture and stick down other, intended whiskers—and decide which are which! He told me once that he found fabric collage about twice as much trouble to frame as any other type of picture and I took his point. The moral in all this is either to learn to frame your own pictures—Prudence Nuttall's 'Picture Framing for Beginners', in the same series as this book, will help you here— or to finish your pictures off very securely before they go to the framer. Do not leave pieces only half stuck down in an airy fashion. If you do, and they come back to you framed in a dis-hevelled state, it will be your own fault. If you do get some foreign body inadvertently framed into the picture, or some piece displaced, it will always appear offendingly obvious when the picture is hanging on your wall.

Make sure your picture has right angles at the corners; a set-square will help you to get the corners squared off. If you have used this correctly, then the measurements at the top and bottom of the picture should be the same, and so should the side measurements. This will be blindingly obvious to any mathematician, but there may be other careless optimists like myself who omit to use a set-square, and then wonder why one side measures 19" while the other side measures only $17\frac{1}{2}$".

If you want to do an oval or round picture, then I suggest that you get the frame first, trace round the exact size of the oval or circle, and keep rigidly to it.

Try not to let the features of your picture spread too near the edge, or they may get hidden in the framing.

If you have done your picture on a thinnish base material, then it is safer to stick it, or lace it as described in chapter 2, onto hard-board yourself, rather than leave the framer to stick it on with a glue that may show through to the face.

When you have taken off any whiskers or bits of fluff which may be accidentally clinging to the picture, and checked its shape, then I suggest you seal it into a polythene bag until you take it to be framed.

Framing

The choice of frames is very much a matter of personal taste. Something of a revolution in framing has been going on in the

Fig. 100 Scotland (with apologies to the Scottish Touring Association)

last twenty years and there are many simple, effective mouldings to choose from—and many appalling ones still around as well. One can learn a lot about good framing by attending as many exhibitions as possible. Gradually one learns to recognise what is effective framing. It is expensive at this stage to make mistakes and better, of course, if one can master the art of framing for one-self.

If you have laced your picture onto hardboard, it could be contained within a box frame, standing away from the mount and frame, as in fig. 26.

A more traditional form of framing, but still very versatile in suiting different types of picture, is that shown in fig. 100. This frame throws the picture slightly forward, with a hessian (burlap) surround 'behind' it. There is something about having a fabric picture surrounded by fabric which is, not surprisingly, very sympathetic. If your picture is gossamer light, like one of Beldy's, then hessian (burlap) would not be suitable. You might choose a concave mount covered in a silk from the picture. A good framer can do this for you.

Fig. 101 Flowers and Birds, by Amanda Heyman (Courtesy Mr and Mrs W. Marlowe)

As a rule, fabric pictures take more kindly to simple frames than to elaborate ones. Ornate gilded carving is more likely to 'fight' with your picture than to enhance it. I very often choose a thin, pale gold frame; it seems to suit a variety of pictures.

You may have an old frame of your own you want to fill. Old maple frames, like the one in fig. 3, are popular, or frames like the moulded one in dull gold framing the delightful 'Flowers and birds' (fig. 101). A slight difficulty here is the basic one that occurs with the framing of all raised collage pictures: before you put it into the frame, you will have to surround the picture with a fillet of wood to prevent the glass from crushing the picture. With a completely flat fabric picture the fillet of wood is not necessary and you can then have non-reflecting glass if you wish. If you place non-reflecting glass a fraction of an inch away from the picture, the picture will appear very diffused.

Perhaps the worst drawback of doing lots of fabric pictures is that, if they are to be preserved, they must be framed under glass. They cannot just be stacked like oil paintings. If you are prepared for them only to last for a year or two, then you can hang them like banners from cords as in fig. 39 (page 35). But, unlike embroidery, fabric collage is quite unsuitable for cushions or garments.

If your children start turning out collages with dizzy enthusiasm and your purse cannot possibly stand the strain of framing them all, then one alternative is to cover them with acetate or transparent 'Libra' film, taken round to the back of the picture and there secured.

Hanging

People hold differing and often strong views on whether fabric pictures mix happily with oil paintings and watercolours in the same room. One solution is to hang them in an entrance hall or on the stairs or landing. You will then constantly be seeing them from different angles and you will capture one of the diverting qualities of fabric pictures: their ability to change in different lights and from different angles, as separate facets of fabric show up. So, to an even greater extent than with paintings, you will have to experiment widely to find just the right place to show your picture off to best advantage. A picture that looks commonplace in one setting will look striking when well lit against the right background colour.

My personal feeling is that apart from halls and stairs—and children's rooms, which are a special case—fabric pictures are particularly welcome in kitchens and bathrooms. But I know people who have decorated their bedrooms and sitting rooms around a fabric picture with tremendous success. If I were doing this, I think I would cover the walls in a textured wallcovering such as grass-paper or linen in a colour suggested by the picture. I would light the picture with a spotlight, and some of the drama inherent in a fabric picture should then lend excitement to the whole room.

For further reading

Creating in Collage by Natalie d'Arbeloff and Jack Yates. Studio Vista, London, Watson-Guptill Publications, New York.
Fabric Pictures by Eugenie Alexander, Mills and Boon Limited, London.
Embroidery and Fabric Collage by Eirian Short, Pitman, London.
How to Make Collages by John Lynch, Thames and Hudson, London and Viking Press, New York.
Picture Framing for Beginners by Prudence Nuttall. Studio Vista, London, Watson-Guptill Publications, New York.
Introducing Fabric Collage by Margaret Connor, Batsford, London.

Index